MAP OF LOST CUCKOOS

# MAP

# OF

# LOST

# CUCKOOS

*James Simpson*

ACTAEON PRESS 2021

First published in 2021 by
Actaeon Press
3 Bakersfield Cottages
Hoyle Lane
Heyshott
West Sussex
www.actaeonpress.wordpress.com

This limited edition hardback
contains seventeen especially
commissioned woodcuts
from Carolyn Trant,
which commemorate the
bicentenary of William Blake's
seventeen engravings
for Thornton's Virgil

This edition limited to 404 copies
the first 101 copies numbered
and signed by the poet.

Copy no . . .

Text © James Simpson 2021
Images © Carolyn Trant 2021

ISBN 978-0-9548385-3-9

A CIP Catalogue record of this book is available
from the British Library

Printed and bound in Great Britain
By TJ Books, Cornwall

*for Cynara*

# CONTENTS

## Hunting the Wren

# Wind from the North

# The Untenanted Room

# Hay-Rattle Ballads

# Blind Tiger

# Hunting the Wren

*She turns as if to go,*
*Half-bird, half-animal.*
*The wind dies on the hill.*
*Love's all. Love's all I know.*

Theodore Roethke

11

# HUNTING THE WREN

I have pressed my forehead against the page
to find the silence in the gutter's splashed overflow,
I heard his murmurings through sycamore
and the first signs of rain.

I have seen his carved faces, his feathered crown,
but he is there in the hollows beyond arm's length,
the last rabbit in the warren,
the hair tuft on the wire.

Where, where is this nightjar,
lost in the tube station
silent in the graveyard
past autumn and the longest winter?

Some burst corpuscle in the brain
blotted him out, just those strange
lost eyes staring from the vaulted ceiling
hidden behind the pulpit's sacked stone.

Like the innocent boy who sits in confusion
trying to find the answer to the sum of words,
as if there is an answer in the taste of carbon,
beginning all things, on his tongue,

in the smoke and grasses;
a reminder of himself,
in the fire cracked flint,
in the chalk turning.

# CHANCTONBURY RING
# IN DECEMBER

The crescent waits;
as moon shifts cloud
tumbling from the water wheel.

The stonechat has pecked the bones
of this sag down -
that lies brittle skinned
grilled by glassed air -
and huddles expecting
a new sacrifice.

Mocked in its faded robin cloth
but keener,
to scour these hills,
to take the life
which hangs within

the lope cattle, that heave in
ushered breath the frozen wind.

# FLINTS ON STEYNING DOWN

These are the stones of sleep
placed here when drowsiness settles the mind.
The rubbed vertebrae, hip bones,
polished carrion of the down shoulder;
part of some fractal,
affine repetition of the chalk giant's throw outs.

Scattered on the hill's arc, set strange
above the cropped turf, they seem to mark
some pattern with the sky.

A map of the constellations perhaps?
Or our soul adrift from the greenery of earth.

# BEHEADING BIRDS

I spent two days beheading birds
cutting free wing and claw for the display case,
cradling frozen lump stone bodies
matted feather, iced to flesh.
Only claws and wings to survive
and the strange heads
giving back their dead eyes.

I boiled the heads
so that flesh would part
be rid from bone.
And the brew stank
of the death it had collected.

There is an unknown eye,
blank, not even glass
and there are tongues floating
caught in the scud
in the phlegm I have made.

Sometimes in sleep
I cannot see past the pleading
but cut into sinew
into bone, wrench,
twist, twist hard,
and I have a child's head in my hands
with a magpie eye.

# THE ASHEN TREE

*for Jeremy Hooker*

The night is full of wires and signals
which cause an entanglement of air.
Motes glister the bowl that hold the badger skull
and yarrow stalk. Bowl burnished with a pebble
and the back of a spoon, fired in a pit
of green pine and birch, to colour a flame.

Will I cross the water, or watch spirits
wave silently from their grave places
on a far-off shore? There is no sin;
only our inability to hear a god
within, or without; the tuning fork,
each wildfire spark, a breath, a resonance.

Blackbirds are hurrying dawn before them
lighting darkness's listless paradox,
and earth settles like dust. Are we also
the boundary line, marking our place
of familiarity apart
from the region where all theories fail?

Let us enter the graveyard near the town centre,
quiet amidst the traffic and hubbub,
to find the homeless man who walks the earth
bare, a bare ring trod, a perpetual 'O'.
He wrings his hands raw, walking his circle
like a leopard pacing the perimeter

of its cage, like the hare poisoned to madness
chasing her scut, running the ground barren.
He is fleeing the hound in his mind,
orbiting a heart point, swinging
on the tattered ribbons of a maypole,
round and round what he is bounded by.

# ELEGY FOR A TENTH CENTURY FARMER

The hill has had its scalp scraped off
and sod, and thyme, and burnet
dry out inside the digger's bucket,
only the bone of the hill
pokes through.

A night of bleak rain
has shown the post holes,
thrown up the farmer's ribs
and an urn of human ash
older than even the farmer knew.

They are marking the grave,
taking all that is left of the children,
pulling the spine that wore down on the hill,
wrapping the urn for safekeeping.

More than can be remembered
a thousand seasons of sleeping,
sleeping.

# BLACKBIRD

I

Sometimes his eye seems
like the black centre of things,
a dying star surrounded,
sun piercing cloud.
He is certain of his expression,
made in his song,
the blade yellow of beak.

II

That unsure arc
shocked like a fairground drop,
as he spun from the car
hit the hard shoulder
flapping.

He is heavier now
full of doubt,
a deep rip in his side
rift of flesh
showing sinews, the yawn of muscle,
split in the firmament.

# THE SANCTUARY OWL

These stones do not seek to quell the Owl's voice
but throw it out again
to sound as the bell sounds
of longing between light and dark.
What brings this bird to sanctuary
when all of sky lies open
wide as the night's gape
under a bristling moon?

'Heloy! Heloy!'
Who knows this cry
that echoes here within the nave
a cone's fall in the belly of the forest?
For the Owl has a man's voice
Heloy, Heloy lama sabatnye.

## SEA STONES

I would make you out of bits of the sea
so I could throw you back again
pebble by pebble.

But you are some creature,
some bird of prey,
a sparrowhawk
picking at the foreheads
of my song birds.

All these pretty skulls
around your roost,
left overs of encrusted wings,
down from warbling throats,
they add to your own
feathered sheen,

but I did not mean you
to be such a free thing,
to kill so indiscriminately.

I should have made you
from bladderwrack,
fishing line, gristles of bait;
fashioned together whelk shells
and mermaid's purse,
used skin of a dogfish
and stones from the sea.

# LAST NIGHT

And when you died from me
I stood among braced pines
listening to the scant wind.

Beneath the sky's furnace
echoing the coughing owl
I found you there

and covered your bracken skin
with all our witnesses;
anointing your eyelids with moth dust

and the goatsucker's black winged lope.
Under the arc of sheet lightning
you rested on shivering heather

gathering your breath
and then you were gone out into the night
beyond my reach.

## NIGHT SKIN

Swimming naked for the first time,
you felt surprise at the sea's cold the rush inside,
as you kicked your legs
like a newborn in the pebble night.
A kale moon, baldy skulled,
your skin of ash and the white-faced owl,
and you a sea owl
from the hole in the yew
and the hole of night
stretching one wing low;
quiet the sea moon,
still the spinner moon
with its rusted hooks.


These are the liquids that eddy and catch,
pour forth from us, flush between
our membranous selves,
like steam rising from a horse's back,
evaporating at first ghost
but unseen even in the ribbing of leaves.

# FALCON

Above the stomach of the sea
with her execrating talon,
ignoring the scatter of gulls,
in silence,
in single-mindedness,
blunt winged
fracture from the cliff.

Something like the gathering of children
to the tide's edge,
pinned fascination
to what is out there,
then circling, circling,
falcon becoming
the sky's molten god,
dissolving gently
to a dark arc
of winnowing beats.

Even as the sun's watery eye,
black masked
she is speaking you
as her dream,
in the day's death,
in the last splitting air

# FIRST HARE

And in the rain is the river also,
its dark shape billowing
in shafts of sluicing water.
I cannot see the scar on my lover's hand
but I know it is there
and kisses sound distant
like drips from a tap
and the suck of the sea's retreat
from rock pools.
What taste was her skin after rain?
I only remember the river
like a bulge-eyed hare
skittering the down
and the hare's blood on my hand,
wanting to keep the mark
of that uncertain baptism.

## SHE DREAMS WELL
## THE DARK SANCTUARIES

She dreams well the dark sanctuaries
the pretty tracery between branches

over ink roads and glazed woodlands
flying the night's open mouth.

She is torn fabric from another place,
showing the bare thorn in her hand,

yet always I turn her into flowers.

# PERFECT THUNDER

Who is looking back down the hill
watching my passing?

Is it my love?

What finer limbs has she
like the limbs of the ashen tree.

Is it my love?


A sorrow of lapwings
in the half light
leaping with Orion from the hill.

A leap with a waver in it;

Nothing is hidden,
everything is hidden,
weeping light
weeping dark.

# Wind From the North

*ἅπαντα τίκτει χθὼν πάλιν τε λαμβάνει.*

Euripides *Antiope*

I

One hundred and fifty-six remain
in the ash of the merchant's house;

some struggle, some seem resigned,
some tuck in their knees

to return to their mother's belly.
We dowse for water waiting

for the hazel twig to twitch,
but there are still eight loaves

cut and ready to be sold;
cracked walnut shells in the tavern fireplace.

II

Men with mattocks
are cutting
into the cuckoo hill;
the place they say
befitting of maidens.

Wheatear, wheatear,

                  from one tussock to another;
horse smatch, fallow lunch,

              from there to the other.


They are breaking open
the mound
with bare hands,
some with axes;
to find a child woven,
swaddled and swollen.

Wheatear, wheatear

              from here to another;
stonechacker, snorter,

              from there to the other.

Brushing soil
from the baby's face,
resurfacing again;
like an owl drowned
in a cattle trough,
through the lutterings
and lettings of rain.

Wheatear, wheatear

                    from one burrow to another;

horse masher, jobbler

                    from here to the other.

And somewhere
in the chalk, in the folds
of her shawl;
three riders
on a bronze bull.

White arse, white arse

                    from here to the other;

clodhopper, chichell

                    from the dead to our mother.

Shaking the buried grain,
cradling the infant
like a hare
laid in a field
which comes
alive again.

III

Cyclamen petals
on window sills
fade in exhaling light.
The hills have horses;

riderless
they graze freely
without the
paraphernalia of war.

And now
and again
they look up
from the bracken;

while women
bend attentive
sponging pale limbs,
talking in whispers.

IV

There is no weeping for the death of a fox;
                              fur flat with rain,
shrunk over hunched ribs:

propped against a fence post,
                              almost casual in its demise;

but without that warm black mollusc of a nose.

It is raining again from the north,
                              wind weaving flocks
of birds like withies;

an immigrant host, massed sodden heads,
                              pick through stubble
and red earth.

Where the barbel sit is bloody with soil;
                              and the river lays sediment
over new wheat.

November's bonfires rest unlit,
                              too late to encourage the sun;

the dead have been drawn back to the dead
                              and the bull is buried.

# The Untenanted Room

*I saw the forest and I saw the land;*
*I looked for marvels, but I could not find them.*

Wace

for Lindsay Clarke

I

We have come to this place
where we kill all gods and dreams,
something inconsequential
scribbled in the margin of our lives.

We write words, but words lie forgotten,
throats are cut, voices taken
and in a glance of life
we trample everything underfoot,
scrabbling to reach the chamber door.

Where oh where is the greenstick boy?
Who has heard the night bird's song?
Even the frosts are gone and the old grain
does not seem to grow anymore.

## II

The bee is in the playground,
come down from the hill of neither mist nor rain:

she is sizeable; queen of a thousand worlds,
conjuring all the flowers from the meadow;

plantain and buttercup,
vetch's purple labia.

Have you walked this way
from the borders of the full sea;

your saffron hair with many tongues,
too many faces imploring God's pardon;

Have you passed this way before,
your arms like the burning

may blossom, crackling
blackthorn, sparks of elder.

A psalm for the plum's late bloom,
a psalm for the ivy flower's remaining sweetness;

a world of cares without understanding,
like a broken song thrush

whistling from its cardboard box;
punctured holes of light to sing for.

He killed the bee; no reason,
just out of place within these walls.

III

She learnt to hate
the blessed birds,
to save his heart from bird song.

At night whilst her son slept,
she would tear down
swallows' nests from under eaves;

sorting through the mud and straw
to find each egg
and best of all, those nestlings

who hadn't flown;
to squeeze their fragile heads between
her thumb and forefinger.

Every nest she ordered to be pulled down,
dove, and woodpecker,
thrush both missle and song.

Yet in the small hours she would lie awake,
waiting for the owls she loved,
listening to their soft calling.

IV


I covet the fire in him;
he is like spring light
on a winter bourne,
the first conjured sun.


Such beauty in the thundering hooves;
the fire, the fire,
shattering sparks,
struck from the forge.


To be him;


like the great roar
of a yuletide burn,
like the beacon's flame
on the hill's back.


To be him.


Notice now the blood
hole in his chest,
my spear was always
an effective weapon.


Somehow he is dimmed:

It is as if he has walked too many miles
and the dust forms a lacquer on his hair;
eyes rimmed with salt,
paper thin, no tears left.

What is there to be said
about the awkward angle of his limbs,
as if his tripod has collapsed,
his hanging cage of ribs
rocking with the last sliver of breath.

What an audience he has.

V

Sift, sift my love
and take a snatch of honey
in your mouth.

The bees come to suckle you,
husk upon little husk,
it is a mean breath they offer.

Shh, there are no flowers
bless the rain on summer bowers,
let me tear each leaf in three

to twine around my fingers;
bind and unbind to find an end,
this the art to which I am given.

Lullay, lullay my little liking
let me cradle you in this shroud
like a leveret in his coffin.

VI

Gods lived here once
and men;
great works
scraped the sky
but the roofs fell in;
ripe skins burst
like a carcass bloated
in the sun;
even the flies have left
turned and run.

Gods lived here once
and men;
but the walls crumbled,
roads ruptured;
how quickly the gold lipped
turn grey;
broken into rubble heaps;
wall braces, iron piling
mangled, contorted to the abstract;

someone laughed here once
on this street corner;
saw the moon
in a pale day
and smiled;
all have passed away.

Here is the empty place,
the untenanted space
where no dweller dwells.
We are that place
not properly inhabited,
swept clean, adrift, cut off,
hung on the grid of numbers.

VII

A thin place in a thin time;
the blood bracked shuddering
in all the glass night;
and we the taut marchers and frost merriers

clasped onto earth's compass
and the crest capped haunches;
singing nights' crystal
and the ward welled blessing.

Through night's branches, gleaming
like starlings, over hillsides
and the breast papped chalk-lands,
lighted like candles and guttering torches.

Ours is the singing of the antlers blazing,
ours is the claim of the boar tusk whittling,
freeing the midden of the oak tree island,
singing the night and the unforgetting.

## VIII

The sky is salt clear, a wave on ebbed air
bringing them in. Rook, jackdaw, ragged crow,
rising to their favoured place;
a single leafless tree:

                      like a dressing of torn cloth.


He has no idea; walking blithely
through this world, the story seems lost to him.
Every step is a wound;

                how adept he is
in his own singularity.
Each crushing step; 'It's not me, It's not me.'


The tree draws them back;

                throws them out again.
He gets up stunned;

         the hammer blow of a beak
still echoing in his head.


      Then the calls,
like women, like his mother, telling him
      again and again.


Another smack;
like being slapped round the face;
         then another.


Clam breaker, nut cracker, cover your eyes.

He can feel the cool calm blood in his hair.
His arms are being pummelled, his fingers picked raw;

there are so many tearing at him now,
he has the taste of metal in his mouth.

He laughs at himself like one who knows
he is dying;

A chuckle.

       And for a moment the birds pause.

Swift, with all his reserve he
                       slaps back a crow;
the bird wheels in the air,
                       thuds to the ground,
a lame bundle.

The cawing stops.
                Only wind in the trees.

Before him a woman lies wounded;
her naked body curled like a shell.
He is on his knees.
                  What has he done?

He has no idea.

## IX

A dream I dream over:
like a fragment of touch
when a lover leaves for the last time;

hoping for a look back
down the hall. The hunted fox
heavy with cubs, run to distraction;

at last the supplicant, tongue lolling,
sitting, waiting, as the circle closes in.
Through the wood's bone cage,

through the orphaned trees,
stars seem like bare knuckles;
for she is gone, vixen to the night,

her cubs left mewling, blind.
Such a sudden birth;
the circle shrinks closes in.

Each cub, one by one,
lifted from the earth, their necks wrung;
but she is elsewhere, teats aching.

X

We could give you many heirs;
hanging from our black dugs
they would be worth a score
of thin boned progeny.

Such fine white throats we have
but we go by different names;
nettle creeper, hay sucker, muffit
and wheetie why; great peggy, meg cut throat.

You view us like a page from a newspaper:
what do you make of these photographs;
dead children wrapped in their mother's shawls,
picture on picture, death with no privacy?

Do you even ask the question?
Instead you fashion a shrunken world
where flickering screens survive
as some form of justification.

And in the end a lone white bear
is pawing the ocean, swimming in circles;
the last leaf of the arctic
drifting towards dark.

XI

There kneels God's knight,
his mind on other things:
blood specks the snow, a few

drops, the spoor of some dainty creature.
What is he looking at;
does he see something I do not?

One poor beast picked from the undulating line;
a clatter goose washed from the watery flood,
sunk far into the ocean streams

but raised living from the waves
by the air and wind,
carried far over the seal's back.

Such attention for a few drops of blood;
I was hanging out the washing;
hopeless really, no chance of anything

drying in such low cloud.
Then I heard them, the stubble geese;
a low clamour somewhere in the mist;

a growling chorus; many souls
talking at once; trying to say something;
but I could not understand what was missing.

XII

I have marked the dead seasons
one by one;
heard footfalls fall again,
fall in a night

so dark, that hills and sky
were one in sound
and still; but for the unusual air
twisting in the beech leaves.

What mysteries are these?
This mouthpiece uttering
the moon's limed walls.
Honest tongue,

there is nothing to be said:
this is the time of candle care
when frost lays
bitter the partial ground;

the lark has spun
the world on its axis;
and the blood
we have shed is mutual.

XIII

I do not know how to speak;
but dreams sift
into the waking mind,
intangible,

yet physical;
as the cuckoo's voice
somewhere in the goat willow.

Not there;
in the distance,
beyond earshot;

not there; out of reach,
inside the dream,
beyond the dream.

Passing away,
in the distance;
only a memory.
I do not know how to speak.

XIV

I have seen the battle of the years;
so I shall turn again into a hare
and shed my skin for this the final time.

The fields are silent; something is missing:
the corn crake in the pea-thistle;
the ebbing lapwing, the skylark's high fury.

Once a man talked of casting seeds;
but he is lost now
at the edge of understanding.

Let there be left a scatter of feathers
as when the fox carries off its prey:
a final moult to mark my dwelling place.

The world has had its play with me:
I shall lie low hidden in the earth's furrow;
until, until this time has had its lot with all.

# Hay-Rattle Ballads

*or*

## Some Light Remains

# THE RHYME

## OF THE

## REDDLEMAN'S DAUGHTER

### IN SEVEN PARTS

for Olwen May

### I

Wine berry, ta diddle, wagtail, den,
   he counted as he walked;
to the spring of St Catherine
   which bubbles from the chalk.

Yellow flag, buttercup, forget me not,
   he led his horse to grass;
to drink the sharp cold that rippled
   near old Cocking pass.

And there the midges and the bats
   were whirligigging dusk
beneath an ash tree canopy
   where the minnowing stream ran past.

Ragged robin, bittercress,
   rushes black and bull
and the worn flints that lay below
   the water chuckling full.

Underneath a homely ash
   he built a fine campfire;
and a ribbon of smoke and scaddle sparks
   drifted higher and higher.

He unhitched a tin bath from his cart,
   filled it from the spring,
and steaming water from his kettle,
   he lifted and poured it in.

Then he picked his daughter up,
   his lovely poppet dear,
and popped her in the piping bath
   a cloud pond still and clear.

'Too hot', 'too hot' she laughed aloud,
   so he stirred it round and round
and a rust red stain washed from his hands
   as a memory unwound.

And then she spoke, like a bright bell,
   like a cuckoo's voice in May,
as the sun dew lipped its afterglow
   at the compline of the day.

# II

'I'll tell a story from my mouth
   of a dream I dreamt Oh daddy dear
and the world it was a sorrow place,
   when child and man had sunken face
and the earth was dust and drear.

From East to West and West to East
   no shred of grass would grow;
and all the trees had been stripped bare
   and the winds had ceased to blow.

Ash and chestnut, elm and beech
   were lifeless standing things
and dry dead twigs were rattling
   like a thousand golden rings.

Every crystal chalk stream
   was a dust dry ridden track;
no sweet sucking from the trout pools
   or beaded otter back.

No beasts that crawl upon the earth,
   no moths or butterflies,
no spiders or slow pulsing worms,
   no birds to mark the skies.

A throng of people gathered
   imploring God on high
but no god was there to hear them,
   he'd left them bye and bye.

Little children cried aloud
   through the stagnant air;
asking why the world was barren,
   like a bone picked bare.

And their mothers and their fathers
   could not look them in the eye;
they'd eaten every living thing
   that could walk, or crawl or fly.

Then it seemed that all the people
   were calling out as one,
a million, million, raw swollen tongues
   clacking at the sun.

## III

Who saw where she had come from,
   who knew from where she came,
like a green blade rising
   from the buried grain?

I felt the earth was trembling,
   and like a split hillside,
a giantess stood there,
   with barley straw for her hair
as a turning tide.

She stood alone amongst them,
   a bursting corn sack moon
and her eyes they had a sadness
   a honeysuckle gloom.

Her tears were those of one who loves
   but knows of what will be,
like a willow weeping quietly
   like a wind-blown tree.

She gathered them up gently,
   in ones, and twos and threes
and gnawed their limbs,
   and stuffed them in,
her stump teeth chewed,
   her gristle food,
with a jaunce and weary grin.

## IV

A gaunt procession shuffled along,
   man, woman, sunk eyed child,
like a sow devouring her farrow,
   her eyes were wide and wild.

Her work went on; on and on,
   on into the night,
the moon rose in the dead sky
   guttering a torn moth light.

The moon it hung, a plucked out eye,
   and her work went on and on;
her feeding was swift now
   as swallows before a storm.

At last, no tears; her tears were gone
   and now her work was done;
she hugged herself shivering,
   huddled cold and dumb.

Then with her nails she raked her face,
   until she drew blood;
and then she tore her barley hair,
   in ragged clumps
with bits of scalp in clotted lumps,
   until her skull was bare.

And in her grief the giantess
   laid on the earth and died;
no living thing was left there
   but dust and sand and stillborn air;
for age on age the addled air,
   and the rocks beside.

# V

Time blinked; and in the distance
   I saw a whirling wind;
far out on the horizon,
   I saw a whirling wind!

And I could hear a little thing
   full hearted like a wren;
deep in the swirling of the storm,
   a droplet diadem.

There somewhere inside the wind
   a ripple in the light;
like a mirage, like water's fire,
   a whirlpool of the night.

Stepping from the spinning winds,
   the twisting sands and dust,
a tiger walked and padded forth,
   singing a dawn chorus.

The tiger padded through the waste
   his shimmering sides a glare,
singing a mournful elegy
   of what had gone before.

# VI

Such a song I never heard
  or ever will again;
like the lonely voice of a green plover
  or longed for summer rain.

And then I saw a precious thing
  for where his footprints lay,
grew up some white dead nettle
  like the dawning of the day.

And with his song of sweet lament
  a mourned for long dead choir;
new living things sprung from the earth,
  a birch bark kindling fire.

I saw the place where the roebuck lay,
  I heard the vixen's cry;
and I marked a flock of jackdaws
  across the southern sky.

And with his song of utmost joy,
  hazels grew gold and green;
as a heron misted northwards
  over dew cobwebbed hornbeams.

Yellowhammer, woodlark,
　grey partridge and quail,
were calling from the grasses
　the cocksfoot and foxtail.

The eel within the spring pool
　curled in its bed of leaves;
and silver-washed fritillaries
　gilded the woodland eaves.

VII

And I awoke on the high blown down
  with swallows above my head
and I did not know if these things had been
  or were to come instead.

And I awoke not knowing,
  if the tiger would sing once more;
if he would call us back again
  as he had done before.'

There under the homely ash
  the Reddleman's daughter yawned;
'Have I dreamed a dream, oh Daddy dear,
  of how the world was born?'

He stirred the dying embers,
  while the hoolets screeched and knelled,
as his daughter turned to sleeping
  sound as a clucket bell.

By the last of the fire,
  he wondered at what was said;
as its tiver glow passed from her face
  and he carried her to bed.

Wine berry, ta diddle, wagtail, den
  he counted as he walked;
leading his horse, up the scarp slope bare,
  onto the hills of chalk.

# HEYSHOTT HARVEST

Three gold headed children bent in prayer,
sun through the west window on the copper ear
of barley, marking Cobden's seat, which we keep free.

Loaves on the altar, a sermon of worlds
in a hazel nut; and the new vicar said
she would not bless the bread, as it was inanimate.

Well up til now, we have blessed a loaf each year
which was kneaded with love, to remember the harvests
when there was no bread, and flour was made

from potatoes and sawdust, as Cobden said.
But it seemed less than nought as the bread
had been bought from a supermarket.

Deuteronomy and the bread of life,
and there still remains a westerly light
on the altar and the corn and the starched altar cloth,

placed with apples from the village orchards;
Braddick's Nonpareil, Knobby Russet,
Blenheim Orange, Peasegood Nonesuch.

# MAP OF LOST CUCKOOS

*for John Burnside*

Every Spring from Hoe Copse to Tegleaze I hope for their return
and that peewits will spire in Pelly Croft casting roundels before the sun.

When the bluebells of Heyshott Common glow under beech tree,
                                                    lacewing-light,
maybe I'll see a cuckoo on its hawk-barred pinion flight.

No-one seems to mark their passing or walk these deathly ways
and I've watched each years' belittlement which threadbare time displays.

I've been stoppered in the stud-hour beneath a black chalk moon
as a drawn winter light dilutes a vacant winter gloom

and it's then that I remember a migrant company
like a people singing unconfined, a joy from their far country.

I cannot walk to Pot Meadow there are pot-sherds upon my eyes
and I've only moth-like memories of where the thistling linnet flies

but perhaps, say on Dunstan westward, or the wealds of Lavington,
I might hear once more a cuckoo's voice and know this dead-time done.

# IN DEFENSE OF COCKERELS or A COMPLAINT AGAINST THE INCREASING GENTRIFICATION OF THE COUNTRYSIDE

Sir George Chanticleer
had a fine cock a doodle
but the woman next door
thought him quite anti-social.

He would cry with the lark
and the owl in the morning,
for his worship was great
when light came a peeping.

He hollered his heart out
when he saw the first sun
and his feathers were bright
as the rays that he'd sung.

His life it depended on
every new day
and the day would not work
less he cocked his own way.

And the gleam in his feathers
and the gleam in his comb,
were just like the sun
in the bright glance of dawn.

But the woman lacked joy
for the king of the heart,
he is quite anti-social
that morning upstart.

So they killed poor Sir George
put him under the ground
and the sun rose next day
with barely a sound.

# TRIPTYCH FOR THEIR MOTHER

## I  OLWEN MAY

After the cow parsley, after the may,
into midsummer as pierce-eyed
as a sparrowhawk there in the ash;
where your mother returned faithfully
each day, breathing in every part of the tree;
waiting for your silver footfall
and the trefoils that would flower
in the prints you made.

## II  FURSE WILLIAM

Not the angel at the annunciation
but the white owl skirting the borders
of our enclosed world; echoing your cries
for a new time of year.
A blood clot birth wailing for completion,
from the tangled ebb-tide of lapwings,
the silent compliant hare.
Not yet the blackthorn shivering the hedge,
or the sun yolk celandine;
but on the common, first to flower,
your bright gold kisses.

## III LUCIA ESSYLLT

I cut the tree the night before your birth,
before light, before the first snowfall.
In the darkness you were that light,
in the depth of the world,
somewhere in the darkest day;
when earth was frozen tight,
and the moon became a slither of itself
and cloud was like a swimming bear,
when we brought in the tree
and gave you your name.

## AT DIDLING CHURCH

How our children are like the wind
and like September's light diffused.
Leaning on gravestones chattering

like swallows on a wire, sun maples
round them haloed from the west;
while from the wood, the wood oaks hiss,

breathe out then in panning for gold.
And the pit pit wren in the graveyard
like moss in your palm;

and our children playing
on the stones;
part wind, part sun.

# SWEET NELLIE BROWN

Sweet Nellie Brown,
Oh sweet Nellie Brown,
the primrose is bleached
and the sun tilts its crown.
The bees in your hives
are betwixt and between;
they murmur your voice
as of incoming rain,

Oh sweet Nellie Brown.

Oh sweet Nellie Brown,
Oh sweet Nellie Brown,
the mice in your house
under floorboards they sing,
a lament of your passing
betwixt and between;
for the sun is fleeting
right over the down

Oh sweet Nellie Brown.

Oh sweet Nellie Brown,
Oh sweet Nellie Brown,
in your beech hedge the dunnocks
build nests once again
just past your green gate
betwixt and between;
Nellie has dwindled
they mark in their dance
and the bees murmur
nothing will be as it was,

Oh sweet Nellie Brown.

Sweet Nellie Brown,
Oh sweet Nellie Brown,
they've taken a saw
to your crooked apple trees,
to 'open the view',
so there's no need to see
betwixt and between;
the bat folded sleeping
under mistletoed bark
and the glut song thrush
tuning blossomful dark,

Oh sweet Nellie Brown.

# THE ILMINSTER THORN

*A Christmas Carol*

The hawthorn is a bawning tree
That blossoms bright in May
But when our meekling babe appears
It flowers on Christmas Day.

The fox was first with down soft brow,
Then ox with steaming side
And all the beasts from near and far,
Came to our Christ's bedside.

For Christ was born 'mongst dairy straw
With creatures huddled round,
The Dorset ewes and spright jackdaw,
The stubble hare and hound.

When snow is drifting, piled hedge high,
Before sweet Christmas morn,
We'll dance along those snow packed heights
To the dairy soft and warm.

We'll go gathering milk and cream
The night that Christ is born,
Oh we'll go gathering milk and cream
With the flowering of the thorn.

Now each and every Christmas night
They stir in flock and sty
And journey quiet to Christ's thorn tree
'Cross drifts and kindling sky.

So, Gloria in Excelsis!
This night when light is born,
From cockle wren to seven tine stag,
At the flowering of the thorn.

# WOOLBEDING

It is like the scene in the oil painting.
A mother and her daughter
walk into night;

the light from the cottage windows
behind them,
two glimmers of an oil lamp.

And so it is when the world marks time
some light remains;
from candles at the carol supper,

of sheep on the hill
above the church
blinking at the gold cupped moon;

from slow progress
across fields
sorting potatoes and stone.

There is still a light from the window
but it is diminishing now,
only our voices gather in the dusk.

# Blind Tiger

*O let me teach you how to knit again
This scattered corn into one mutual sheaf,
These broken limbs again into one body...*

William Shakespeare   *Titus Andronicus  V iii*

I

An offering of grain;
an offering of drink.
Blind tiger forgive us
for making you a stuffed head;
your jaws set to grimace
for a hundred years;
your eyes as jewels
reflecting the setting
suns of empires.

Is the tiger listening
to the trees?
Place its skull in the river,
force open its jaws,
place a leaf on its tongue.

## II

How many winters
has the tiger endured;
watching with its glass eyes
the decay of shires?

Suddenly, snowdrops in hedgerows;
the child in the birch bark cot
coos to himself.
He is warm in his bed of moss;
in his fish skin clothes.

The wind rattles the claws and teeth
which hang dangling on strings
above the cradle.
Clack of tiger tooth
on bear claw.

# III

Blind tiger your forests are gone
and the rivers silt with effluent.

They have dressed you
in plastic wrappings
and tied bags of excrement
to your tail.

It is better
they pull out your claws and teeth;
leave your feet bleeding,
leave the bloody sockets of your mouth.

Let them drug you,
forever pacing your cage;
until each bone is rendered,
until you are flayed again.

# IV

Blind tiger I have hunted you
in my dreams.
Your wound has left
its blood trace in dust
or on pebbles
by a mountain stream;
mixed in the resin
of tall pines.

I have wondered
at your drowning
in fire and water.

I have stood at the edge
of the wound's dark hole;
the stars are simple here.

V

My mouth is full of birch twigs
and the hills lie in abasement;
only the contaminated earth
and sulphurous rain.

They found your skin
in an out-house;
last of your species
rotten and moth-worn.

Blind tiger, it is not what I expected
when I woke,
to stand on this mountain
as waters rise.

Life is ending in a putrid crucible;
and I am here cupping water.

## VI

He lies in shadows;
lies with a woman
whose body is that of a tiger?
The room is silent;
and shadows like stripes
cast across her back.

How can he return home
across moors with the sea fretting;
back to smoke stained tenements,
to a bound suspect God
and the sleeting rain?

Blind Tiger, is it true of angels
that they fail to see through
the unremitting dark?

# VII

Young women in saris
are singing carols;
neon strobes the bedroom ceiling,
the city's traffic is perpetual.

Let us enter the forest at night,
let us go to the place
where they set snares.

In the lamplight
gnats dance a double helix;
someone is singing by a forest stream,
young girls are washing
in a forest stream.

Blind Tiger, these traps were not set by us;
we did not give our consent.

# VIII

Blind tiger you are a foolish god
but our foolishness is greater.

The noise of helicopters
is shaking the dead in their graves,
and children too young to know,
wake startled
by the sound of something
quite inexplicable.

How can the celandine
justify its existence;
as the season rots,
as spring rots;
we shake our heads
with the making of it?

# IX

Who carves you in amber
singing to the trees,
singing to the woman
who breaks bark
revealing the heart wood,
the pith which carries
both water and sun?

I watch the flames
through your eyeholes;

watch the flames
through your tear shaped nostrils.

After love, after beauty,
once the spirit passes,
nothing remains but fire.

X

How to unmake a head?
How to undo the taxidermist's art?

Gifted a portion of God
it is time to peel back
the skin from its scalp,
so that he might require
several appetites,
might require certain
planetary alignments.

Let in only those who love,
the molly-coddlers and embracers,
those who absentmindedly
lift a hair
from your shoulder.

## XI

There are no new stories
to tell our children;
we no longer journey to the mountains;
we have let the tree bleed
too long, slaked and glutted.

The nails have been driven in
flush to their heads
and the wound is purpled.

Un-pin him
so he is no more
a fixed mark;
let him pour
once again *in waves*
*through all things*.

# XII

Amongst the keepsakes
wrapped in a piece of linen:
a slipper limpet,
an oak gall, a lock of hair,
a photograph.

A woman who has lost her love
is trying to catch may petals.

How is it we replace
ourselves each day
from the blank quarter
from the sky's lost quarter?

Venus lies close to the capsized moon
like the bloom of a plum,
subtle to the breath's condensation.

# XIII

Rooks flock in numbers,
small voices
in a birch paper sky.

A fox is seawarding
into shadows,
smell of thrift and milk.

There is a child's voice
in the dusk
and her mother is calling to her,
calling her with care and laughter;
such care that light
is beholden to it,

as the passage of stars
bubble into night.

## XIV

The ant knows
the circumference of things,
the rim of a pygmy shrew's ear
each blackthorn spike.

We lie together
anonymous somewhere
in a city, listening
to footsteps on a pavement
from the street below.

And so we become
a memory
of a sleeping child,
harkened like
the least of angels.

## XV

May I catch you by the ear
Blind Tiger and whisper secrets
to the finery of your skull.

Were you there
when they bulldozed bodies,
when they reduced us to binary numbers,
condensed us to component parts,
to cytosine and guanine,
to adenine and thymine?

Look into the dead child's eye
at the apple colours of the universe.
Take care of your reflection.

Mercy Blind Tiger, mercy;
mercy, mercy, mercy.

## XVI

Blind Tiger, when will we learn
the subtlety of extinction;
only a few have left traces
of themselves behind,
with no intention
anymore than sleep.

What remains
lies deep under corn;
and after harvest, before
the threshing begins,
you stand in stillness
at the forest edge
watching sheaves being gathered,
turning your heart to pollen.

## XVII

He searches for flints,
for bulb fractures, for shatter marks.
A kestrel is rising like
smoke over tumuli.

There are kisses in words,
parcels of silks like petals,
carved wooden gods
with elephant heads.

For in the end he knew
she was the miracle itself,
the secret which every god
refuses to utter,
that we are all,
forever, incarnate.

## XVIII

The days pass when we too turn
to amber, when we too fail
the clotted earth.

Pheasants crank wheel through beech woods,
mist hangs in the long grass
and burnished leaves
journey imperceptibly
through fathomless air.

Behold Blind Tiger
you have been disfigured for us
and carry all our sorrows;

for we are greater
at our method of counting,
allocating numbers to the dead.

## XIX

Where do you come from Blind Tiger;
not from countries or corporations,
nor from the vast plazas of etiquette.

You step into a room
and there is nothing there,
only a dusty chair and table,
an old paraffin lamp.

I see footprints
on the wooden floorboards,
note the weight of your spoor,
such delicate nature in your
splayed footmarks.

We are neither here nor there;
left unfurnished.

# XX

Why do we berate
ourselves with perfection?
This light is not the light of dawn.

Speak plainly Blind Tiger;
stir the great cylinder of Earth
with your loquacious tongue,

build a temple of laurel,
fashion an edifice
of beeswax and feathers,

weld tides within days;
as black larvae pursed
in a web-folded leaf

become everything
the nettle has to give.

## XXI

Blind Tiger, we have searched
for your forgotten parts in the ash spills
and rubbish tips of our cities.

Like a bride seeking her bridegroom
we have travelled to birdless places,
through bluebell woods
at the opening of spring.

We have gone far beyond
the peeled green leaf,
to where flies no longer circle drowsily;
and there is no trace.

Have you become such strange particles;
or will we find your claws and jawbone
so we might piece you together?

## XXII

The flower in the tiger's mouth
is not dissimilar from our own.

*

# ACKNOWLEDGEMENTS

My grateful thanks go to the editors of Agenda, The London Magazine, Resurgence and The Hardy Society Journal who have published many of these poems. *The Untenanted Room* was published as an Agenda Editions in 2011 with woodcuts by Carolyn Trant. *The Rhyme of the Reddleman's Daughter* was published as a pamphlet by Hedgehog Poetry Press in 2019.

I have collaborated with the artist and printmaker Carolyn Trant on several artist's books, *Hunting the Wren (2007)*, *The Rhyme of the Reddleman's Daughter (2015)*, *Some Light Remains (2017)*, *The Untenanted Room (2011 and 2018)* and *Blind Tiger (2021)* all Parvenu Press; editions of which reside in private and public collections nationally and internationally. Actaeon Press have published facsimile editions of *Hunting the Wren (2007)*, *The Untenanted Room (2011)*, *The Rhyme of the Reddleman's Daughter (2018)* and *Blind Tiger (2021)*.

'Woolbeding' won second prize in the Thomas Hardy Society's James Gibson Memorial Poetry Competition. 'The Ilminster Thorn' was written as part of a collaboration with the composer Ginny Barrett and recorded in 2018 by Robyn Stapleton, BBC Radio Scotland's Young Traditional Musician 2014, accompanied by folk musician Alistair Iain Paterson.